LIKE BLOOD ON
THE BITTEN TONGUE

LIKE BLOOD ON THE BITTEN TONGUE

delhi poems

AKHIL KATYAL

art: VISHWAJYOTI GHOSH

cntxt

First published in hardback in 2018 by Context, an imprint of
Westland Publications Private Limited

Published in paperback in 2023 by Context, an imprint of Westland Books,
a division of Nasadiya Technologies Private Limited

No.269/2B, First Floor, 'Irai Arul', Vimalraj Street, Nethaji Nagar,
Alapakkam Main Road, Maduravoyal, Chennai 600095

Westland, the Westland logo, Context and the Context logo are the
trademarks of Nasadiya Technologies Private Limited, or its affiliates.

Text Copyright © Akhil Katyal, 2020
Art Copyright © Vishwajyoti Ghosh, 2020

ISBN: 9789357765695

10 9 8 7 6 5 4 3 2 1

The views and opinions expressed in this work are the author's own and the
facts are as reported by them, and the publisher is in no way liable for the same.

All rights reserved

Typeset by Jojy Philip, New Delhi
Printed at Saurabh Printers Pvt. Ltd.

No part of this book may be reproduced, or stored in a retrieval system,
or transmitted in any form or by any means, electronic, mechanical,
photocopying, recording, or otherwise, without express written permission of
the publisher.

for
Vikramaditya Sahai

Contents

1. He was as arrogant as a — 1
2. तुम कोई मेट्रो स्टेशन होती — 2
3. My grandfather — 3
4. In the Urdu class — 6
5. In the third Urdu class — 7
6. तुम याद आते हो — 10
7. This evening in Delhi — 11
8. Two memories — 13
9. Five things I noticed in the 1807 map of Delhi — 17
10. Khusro and Nizam: a villanelle — 19
11. Maruti Swift — 21
12. Aligarh — 23
13. दिल्ली में घर ढूंढना — 26
14. For someone who'll read this 500 years from now — 28
15. At the National Museum — 31
16. Mathura Road — 33
17. On our last date, when we did not know… — 36
18. We were English-medium kids — 37
19. 'Gurgaon' is now 'Gurugram' — 38
20. वो — 39
21. 'A 20 megaton nuclear bomb will…' — 40
22. Across the river — 42
23. बटवारा जितना भी कर लो — 43

24. In 1950	44
25. A description of people	46
26. Moments before she died	48
27. Birds	50
28. Bangla Sahib	52
29. An evening concert in Connaught Place	53
30. At the swear-in ceremony	55
31. Namesakes	56
32. फासीवाद की सबसे पहली देन होती है	57
33. 'Minuscule minority, Minuscule minority'	60
34. i want to 377 you so bad	61
35. Girl, when you	63
36. [Varun is Typing]	64
37. निज़ामुद्दीन वेस्ट के 'स्टार लुक्स' सलून में	65
38. Things you discover your first day cycling in Delhi	67
39. That evening	70
40. Ghazal	73
41. Nigambodh ghat	74
42. The chandelier in Jama Masjid	76
43. Jama Masjid	79
44. In Delhi, last winter	80
45. Sappho in Delhi	82
46. Limerick for the danger boy	83
47. At the tailor's	85
48. Whenever you see it	86
49. हर रात	88

50. रामजस के मेरे एक शिक्षक मित्र बता रहे थे	89
51. For JNU	90
52. दुआ, इन दिनों	92
53. Delhi summer	93
54. Behind the Lodhi crematorium	94
55. The funeral	95
56. Half an hour	97
57. Indra Vihar	99
58. No one knows there's a sharp precipice	100
59. Outer Ring Road	101
60. Twenty kinds of people on the Delhi metro	102
61. Hip-Hop boy	104
62. At night, I woke up	106
63. The road from Kishangarh	107
64. दिल्ली दी गे पार्टियां	109
65. कदी बेब्बे जी डिग्गे, कदी बाउजी	110
66. तुम्हारी एक sight	111
67. Memory	112
68. Jangpura Extension	113
69. auto ride	115
70. Crossing over Yamuna into Delhi	116
71. Akshardham Temple	117
72. I saw him running behind the 541	119
73. The Barakhamba Road/Tolstoy Marg crossing	121
This is not fair, Bombay	122
75. When	124

76.	When she and I go together	125
77.	One of the last things	126
78.	It is two years before	128
79.	This evening	130
80.	JNU	131
81.	Did you know	134
82.	एक इमरजेंसी का समर्थक	135
83.	Kaanwariyas are good for the night-life of Delhi	136
84.	Near Eros cinema, Jangpura Extension	138
85.	हम हैं दिल्ली वाले जी	141
86.	मुझे बस	142
87.	'But he is pointing his finger at us,'	143
88.	The railway tracks between Jangpura and Lajpat	145
89.	आज	147
90.	तुम आये हो	149
91.	Flow through me	150
92.	Our phone GPS had misled us	151
93.	चाहने से क्या नहीं मिलता	157

Acknowledgements	159
The Poet	161
The Artist	162

He was as arrogant as a

Chattarpur farmhouse but
in the end I figured he was
just cluttered, like Adhchini,
which I liked. Our beginnings
were rocky, we held hands
infrequently and uneasily,
like Def Col and Kotla,
but then, in some years,
often and more breezily,
like Jangpura & Jangpura
Extension. All those years
of romance and apprehension,
he'd held me in his Najafgarh
arms and kissed me like
Shalimar Bagh. Not that we
didn't fight like Rajouri,
crossing each other's Civil
Lines, not that he wasn't at
times distant like Greater Noida,
or quiet like Asola, but always,
when the worst had passed, we
returned at last to where we'd been,
somewhere near Dilshad Garden,
by the blessings of Nizamuddin.

तुम कोई मेट्रो स्टेशन होती

तो ज़रूर येल्लो लाइन पर
'घिटोरनी' होती

इससे कम दमदार नाम
तुम पर जचता ही नहीं

मेरा क्या, मैं तो ऐसे ही ठीक हूँ
तुम्हारे मेरे बीच ये पूरी दिल्ली है
इसलिए आने से डरता हूँ
थोड़ा मीक हूँ

सदा तुम्हारा,
विश्वविद्यालय

My grandfather

would ask us to read him
the shop signs in Devanagari:

मिंटू आइसक्रीम
जगत हार्डवेयर
चित्र सिनेमा

All his life, he
only knew Urdu,
leaving Lahore at 18,
a young railway clerk
new at the desk then.

In the early months
he struggled,
tried opening a cigarette shop
at Panchkuian Road in Delhi,
before being given the same job
in the Indian Railways
in Lucknow.

In all this commotion
he never bothered
learning another script,

dependent still, at 73, on his grandchildren
to read him ice-cream signs
when he treated them to
an orange bar.

Years later,
when I ache to read Faiz's letters
in his own handwriting, I have to
write to a Facebook friend in Lahore,
or ask an old Jangpura neighbour,
or worse, use a translation app,
which is like rubbing stones on silk.

As grandfather and I stumble
through these years,
Urdu, Hindi
still look on at each other
in an old mirror convexed by history,
reaching around its opaque silver.

*

This year,
after my second Urdu class,
I get straight on the Blue Line
—nuqtas arraying in my head—
for the Ramakrishna Ashram station.

Here, in this first city of his coming,
Panchkuian Road, where he tried
but failed at a living, पंचकुइयाँ रोड,
that of the five old Mughal wells,
پنج کوئیاں روڈ, where grandfather and I
after the opacity of years
find homework in a Delhi road sign,
we caress old shapes
into meaning, curve old losses,
draw water with
a new tongue.

In the Urdu class

I confuse my *be* with *pe*.

He asks me to write 'water'
I write 'you'.

Who knew they'd make them so close
Aab (آب) and *Aap* (آپ).

Both difficult to hold on to.

(thanks to Abdur Rehman Khan)

In the third Urdu class

I was introduced to
do chashmi he

ھ

miracle-maker

almond-eyed
bugger

card-trick of a character

it adds weight
to whoever it sits next to

it turns *ba* to *bha*
da to *dha*
ka to *kha*

with the confidence
of a goon

it adds (sometimes)
a glottal spur

—a breath of life—

three ounces and
a whisper

carves the naked wood
of sound

into aspirate
texture.

I wish I had it years ago

—to know exactly
what to add

in what
air-thin measure—

I would've placed it
equidistant
between us.

तुम याद आते हो

जैसे नाईट ड्यूटी पर नींद आती है
बिन बुलाये, हमेशा

This evening in Delhi

when the auto climbs
the Lodhi Road flyover

and the two modernist arms
of the Methodist Church
take God's shape

for that half-a-second
my eyeline swims through
the shikhars of the basti's Shiv temple
straight to the finial—princely green—
of the white-as-milk dome
of the Khilji Mosque

in whose shadow
sleeps Nizamuddin, beloved
of God, *Mahbub-e-Ilahi*, lying here
eight hundred years, he will outlive us
all, our prince, till the half-second
passes, you climb down
just as his dome's white
catches the last of the sunlight
and you realise

one doesn't always have to travel
four hundred thousand kilometres
to reach the moon.

Two memories

I

Laxmi Nagar
(1997)

I must have been twelve
when a granduncle was discovered
during a vacation in Delhi.

You don't know him?
We told you, he's
Nani's eldest brother
(from Sargodha, Pakistan).

I'd never met a granduncle till then.

In his Jamuna-paar house,
he looked so frail sitting
in his drawing room
that I was afraid to go near him.

As he spoke to us,
I followed his closed eyelids
that kept egg whites beneath them.

He could not see.
And for me, his could-not-seeness
froze in the middle of the room
but no one mentioned it.

I tried to measure how much
he could see of the snacks on the table.
After a while
he asked Pinki (my mother's name
for those who knew her longer than I)
to let him see us.

We were asked to go stand
in front of him. I walked slowly, my bones
shaped like question marks.

He touched my face
with his slight fingers,
moving them lightly over my nose,
my eyes (should I keep them closed?
Or open?) and said, 'nice looking'
in English, then let me go.

I bundled back
to my corner of the sofa
to the edge of my mother,
safe from her people,
those who knew her longer than I,

reedy granduncles who saw people
through their fingers.

II

Jangpura Extension
(2016)

Rohit, it has been six years
since you left

and I am beginning
to forget your face.
It is surprising how a few years
without a Facebook friendship
can blur the edges of cheekbones
and fade the eyes to—
were they dark-brown or black?

I can no longer see your DU grin,
or your getting-a-blowjob face
that first morning I slept in
at your Safdarjung house, or
your Brighton seashore yawn.

All have gone,
and each time I try to measure

how much I can see of you,
a detail disappears.

But sometimes
in the thin morning air,
my hand takes the shape
of holding you from the back

as if your shoulder is still there,
the graze of your stubble,
the lemon of your hair,
the soft drip of your ear

and because each passing year
I remember you by skin,
by my fingers digging in,

these nights
I hold you by your chin,
whisper in your ear
'nice looking'
and just saying it holds off the dawn,
it holds off the claim of the next day,
it holds off *who told you to go
why did you have to go,* it holds off
where are you now.

Five things I noticed in the 1807 map of Delhi

1. The British Surveyor's surname is 'White'.

2. He's still using light blue for the 'Jumnah'.

3. The map's scale is emotionally accurate. Every inch is one and a quarter miles.

4. The walled city is light red. In fifty years the colour will be 'bayoneted on the spot'.

5. Where you and I met last night is not on the map.

Khusro and Nizam: a villanelle

'The real causes of the loss of the Mughal Empire were some mistakes committed by the elders of that king [Bahadur Shah], and the biggest of them all was that they had separated lover and beloved from each other, by burying Muhammad Shah between the graves of Hazrat Mahboob Elahi and Hazrat Amir Khusro.'
—*Ahmed Ali,* Twilight in Delhi

They parted them in their graves
for a Mughal to be buried in between.
Khusro and Nizam count the days —

How long before this city's razed?
Part not the lovers, the curse had been,
they parted them in their graves.

Now look from the ridge, all Delhi's ablaze.
'They exiled the king, what do you mean?'
Khusro and Nizam count the days

till Bahadur Shah looks for a little place
to be buried in, far from home, unseen,
they parted them in their graves.

Setting up the marquee, a worker says,
'They're white as milk, the new king an' queen'.
Khusro and Nizam count the days

till the time another Delhi pays
its ransom to the lovers that had been,
they parted them in their graves.
Khusro and Nizam count the days.

Maruti Swift

It takes a 1248cc diesel engine
4 cylinders
16 valves

a max torque of 190 newton metres
@ 2000 revolutions every fucking minute

it takes rack & pinion steering
& drum brakes & disc brakes & steel tyres

it takes one thousand five hundred kilos
of metal moving, always moving
in 48 second loops on the assembly line

painted & cut & bolted & fed by workers.

It
takes
workers

on 9 hour shifts
one 30 minute lunch break
and two 7 minute tea-cum-toilet breaks
(those two-seconds-late-&-pay-cut-breaks)

it takes 'if my leg itches, I do not even
have time to scratch it'

it takes waiting
for one's own fingers

it takes white-hot 'discipline'
cut by teeth welded by metal to townships
with smoke-grey evenings

it takes 13 days of occupation
months of sit-ins, lock-outs
it takes 147 workers
arrested on manufactured evidence
to make one of these.

(Manesar)

Aligarh

On 8 February 2010, two men forced their way into Dr Ramchandra Siras's house and shot a video of him in bed with another man. The next day, Siras, a professor of Marathi literature, was suspended by Aligarh Muslim University for 'gross misconduct'. The courts ruled against the university, giving Siras his job back. On 7 April that year, Siras died in a rented house under mysterious circumstances, a day before the letter revoking his suspension arrived in his office.

Dr Siras,
in those nights
you must have felt loneliness like a drip

the walls of your room
held together by a faint song,
past loves sitting by you
combing the hours.

That poem, Dr Siras,
where you ask the *beloved moon*
not to fear *the dawn that separates us*,
where you seek consolation
even from shadows

I read it last night on the terrace,
it held my hands, *we will dance
as shadows dance*, it let grass grow
under my feet, *we will touch
as shadows touch*, it hurt
my morning into dewdrops.

Dr Siras, in my Delhi barsati
the windows open onto a palash tree.
I was 27 when I first moved into it,
the landlord did not pause
at the word 'bachelor',
he only asked if I had 'too many parties'.
I didn't. I got the house.

But next time, Dr Siras,
when I look for a place in this city
I'll be older (I was born the year
you got your Ph.D.) and they'll
pause at 'marriage'?

I'll try to draw respect from a right surname,
from saying 'teacher',
from telling them my birthplace,
and will try and hide my feeling small
under my feet.

You had said you were always
unseen in the light of day.

What did you say, Dr Siras,
when you looked for that house
in Durga Wadi?

What did you tell the neighbours,
'Teacher', 'Professor', 'Poet'?

What gives us this respect, Dr Siras,
this contract with water?

In those nights,
weighing this word in your hands,
you must have felt weak,
you must have closed the windows
to keep out the evening,
you must have looked back
and hung the song in the air
between refusal and letting go.

(thanks to Apurva M. Asrani, Deepu Sebastian Edmond and Ishani Banerjee)

दिल्ली में घर ढूंढना

कितने लोग रहेंगे?
हम सिंगल लोगों को घर नहीं देते
सिर्फ फैमिलीज़ को,
नहीं मकान-मालिक ज़्यादा रोक-टोक नहीं करता
बस नॉन-वेज और एलकोहॉल नहीं
जैन है न, इतना तो बनता है,
अरे वो तो मुसलमानों का एरिया है, कंजस्टेड है
एक के ऊपर एक
आप मुस्लिम के घर रह लेंगे?
देखिये ग्राउंड फ्लोर आसानी से नहीं मिलता
यहाँ ठीक है, यहाँ सब पंजाबी हैं
पूरा वेंटिलेशन है,
नहीं बैचलर लोग न्यूसन्स करते हैं न, नहीं आप नहीं
वैसे बोल रहा हूँ
आप कहाँ के हैं?
क्या करते हैं?
नाम?
नहीं, पूरा नाम?

For someone who'll read this 500 years from now

How are you?
I am sure a lot has changed

between my time and yours
but we're not very different,

you have only one thing on me:
hindsight.

I have all these questions for you:
Do cars fly now?

Is Mumbai still standing by the sea?
How do you folks manage without ozone?

Have the aliens come yet?
Who is still remembered from my century?

How long did India and Pakistan last?
When did Kashmir become free?

It must be surprising for you,
looking at our time, our lives

must seem so strange to you,
our wars so little,

our toilets for 'men' and 'women'
must make you laugh

our cutting down of trees
would be listed in your 'Early Causes'

our poetry in which the moon
is still a thing far away

must make you wonder, both
for that moon and for poetry.

You must be baffled
that we couldn't even imagine

the things you now take for granted.
But let that be, would you do me a favour

for old times' sake? Would you go to
Humayun's Tomb in what used to be Delhi

and just as you're climbing
the front stairs, near the fourth step

I had cut into the stone wall
to your left—'Akhil loves Rohit'.

Will you go look for it?
Just that. Go look for it.

At the National Museum
(December 2018)

Below an 18th century Mewar miniature
of a lone tiger in a jungle,
the caption reads
'A Tiger in a Jungle'.

Below a 7th century Chinese sculpture
from Xinjiang, of a lady
riding a horse, the caption reads
'Lady Horse Rider'.

Below a late-Mughal flask,
carved, inlayed,
whose belly is made of
small tablets of jade fused together
in gold wire, hair-thin,
and at each joint the gold
turning into jasmine, every petal
a crease on its mineral skin
till it tapers into the white slenderness
of a neck lined with rubies
the colour of hunted Saras eyes—
Who would drink from this neck?
Whose tongue was made to taste

this jade? Whose fingers could hold it?
Who would summon it full with blood-red
wine, follow its gold line to their lips,
who could behold it?
Who'd even dare to ask?—
the caption reads
'*Surahi* (Flask)'.

Mathura Road
(11 p.m.)

The night is written
in a script I don't understand.

The pavement
is a long hopscotch
of tiles and beer bottles.

A black river flows under.

As I count my steps
the red of a bus grazes
my shoulder.

The number plate
carries the quote: 'The night
is fattened goat. The night
is evil eye'.

I keep walking. More night-buses
whiz by with the quick wisdom
of roads.

This is a small stretch.

This is a small stretch
of an old road
from Chittagong to Kabul,
bruised by old feet.

I keep counting steps.

An emperor lies buried
by the wayside. And a poet
whose wisdom was quicksilver.

I walk past his epitaph.

Behind me now,
Rahim lies wrapped in the muslin
of his aphorisms.

Seeing me, he settles against
his headstone

and asks one couplet
to take off its clothes
'रहिमन धागा प्रेम का...'

he asks another to
jump off the bridge
'...मत तोड़ो चटकाय...'

a third one, he sends after me
with premonitions of rain
'...टूटे पे फिर न जुरे, जुरे गाँठ परी जाय।'

It is getting late. I turn
back. The knot remains.

As I leave him behind
his skin is breaking into marble.

On our last date, when we did not know, we walked over a railway bridge
Paharganj to Ajmeri Gate

Under your feet
the trains left for *Lucknow,*
for *Shakurbasti,* for *Jhansi,* for *Gaya*

I'd held your hand, uncertainly, all evening

Under my feet
they were leaving for *a gamble,*
for *a town of debt,* for *a shadow,* for *gone.*

We were English-medium kids

We grew up in Lucknow, Delhi,
Calcutta, but read in schools,
old English fools who spoke of
seasons that didn't exist—'Shall
I compare thee to a summer's day?'
left us more than a little confused,
yes of course, if you insist, but
something inside us still refused,
have you ever lived a Delhi summer,
'coz if you do, you won't woo with
that line unless your love's a bummer.

'Gurgaon' is now 'Gurugram'

The idea is BJP's
They say it's for Guru Dronacharya
Eklavya be like 'B****, please!'

वो

1948
में जन्मा,
मतलब पूरा
पाकिस्तानी, कोई
बटवारे से पहले का
नहीं कि किसी भी तरह
उसको अपना बता लें। पर
दिक्कत ये है, कि उन सब रातों
को कैसे भुलाएं जब हम उसकी
आवाज़ में घुलते जाते थे, 'आफ़रीं
आफ़रीं' सुनके, तब नहीं पता था नुसरत
हैं उनके।

(Delhi, 2016)

'A 20 megaton nuclear bomb will create a firestorm covering 6500 sq. km...'

and over days and weeks, a black cloud will keep spreading till it covers vast swathes of the subcontinent

'...ye Diwali ke liye rakha hai kya'
—Prime Minister Narendra Modi, April 2019

'...hamne koi Shab-e-Baraat...ke liye rakhe hue hain ye'
—Former President Pervez Musharraf, June 2015

Distance between Delhi and Lahore: 409 km

Distance between Delhi and Lahore
on Diwali: 409 km

Distance between Lahore and Amritsar
on Shab-e-Baraat: 50.2 km

Shab-e-Baraat
'the night of forgiveness'

Distance between Amritsar
and Sargodha (where Nani was born): 276 km

Sargodha: where she did not return.

Diwali is
'the night of return' 'the night of lights'
is Shab-e-Baraat.

The bomb, when dropped, is blinding light
hotter than the sun.

Across the river

—the king's door—
Shahdara

and to the north
—a garden retreat—
Shalimar Bagh

with GT Road's two millennia old
bitumen cutting through
its skin, within

which a walled city
holds together somehow, sleeping in,
crushed between Kashmere
and Mori Gate, not far

from a river, which
every year, turns into a pity

you'd have guessed the city
by now, if you're a shrewd billi—

is it, is it
Lahore or Dilli?

बटवारा जितना भी कर लो

गर्मी लाहौर दिल्ली दोनों में पैंतालीस ही पड़ेगी

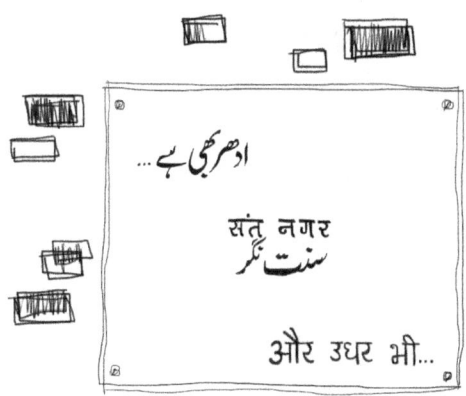

In 1950

CP was 17.

Then one night, Krishna Sobti —striped pants, black shirt & don't-fuck-with-me spectacles— orders a coffee at Wenger's, notices the bandmaster's 'very polished' shoes, she approves, winks at the cup and makes her move, asks him to play that country classic—*My shoes keep walking back to you*. His smirk knows she's flirting. He begins to play it 'just for you!' Under their feet, the night is keen.

A starling splits the arches.

CP turns 18.

(with thanks to Trisha Gupta)

A description of people
(December 2018)

for Jyoti Pandey

I remember that day
six years back, exiting
the CS metro station and stumbling
into a sea of feet. The sky was
an odd, intrepid blue.

A few days before,
a bus near Munirka had stumbled
into black, making the city
grow a new limb
of people.

At Rajpath, the first thing I see—
a girl has climbed up a lamp-post,
she has caught the South Block
between her forefinger and thumb
and her shout has licked the sky clean.

Below her,
nine schoolgirls, in uniform,
have come after a FB post had told them—
'If not now, then when; if not you,

then who'. One of them carries a polythene bag
with a water-bottle, two text books
and anger.

Behind them, a group of four women,
fortyish, friends, black armbands and
plastic green bangles on their wrists,
look up at the lamp-post, cheer the girl on
and eat the salt of her air.

Riding past them on a black Pulsar,
two boys, early twenties, kalawa-wristed
(on the number plate, letters, numerals
and caste name) race up and down
the road, looking quizzically at the banner
that says something about Manipur.

A journalist files her report,
saying into the camera 'Yes, the crowd
is mostly middle-class but…'

Next to her, a DU girl carries a banner that
asks for the moon for her city.

Around her, a few thousand
write 'Justice' on the asphalt

as the water-cannons
are readied behind them.

Moments before she died
(29 December 2012)

It is the night of foreboding

her skin is again
translucent

and all the past is a story
without a moral

this night refuses to rest
on little promises

recalling again the promise,
the coral stone of a world
very different from the one we live in

this night remains
like shell-shock

lies like a fetter—
this waiting for bad to get worse
for it to get better

this night hangs in the air
like the deserter
who has seen through the war,
his world is now refusal

(that night, the first thing she asked
when she was conscious again
was whether they had been caught)

she lived each moment she died
each

and this night remains
because she has offered her sleeve to hold
but we are not bold enough
to reach.

Birds

as evening clouds gather over Ajmeri Gate

the kite forgets
its way home
in the wind

a myna feather scales
seven storeys of a carpark
on its own

the first drop
on the stone
of Ghaziuddin's tomb
curls its marble into irises

its nest mussed by water
the black drongo—*kotwal*—
enters the madrassa classroom,
takes a lesson
in rain

a school-boy finds shelter
under a pilkhan tree

two hundred years before,
his paint-brush edged

on the final ivory
of graves, Sitaram
paints everything he sees
stones, trees, domes, filigrees
—like Lady Hastings ordered—
everything but the crow
walking sanguinely
over the dead

Bangla Sahib

The Delhi night is full,
the moon sits on high.
The road is grey with
the remains of the day,
those who walk by, see

Bangla Sahib

sending
gold
into
the
sky.

An evening concert in Connaught Place

(*September 2019*)

His hands on the mridangam
were long exposure

a finger-haze

— as the vocalist skeined
the night into song —

he played
with his shoulder-blades

cutting each note
with goatskin

his fingers dying
on the membrane

each stroke
an afterlife of limb.

The song breaks
over us —

Lal Ded wrestles
with a lion.

In the hull of the mridangam
a silence is clamped
by leather straps

like on a people.

At the swear-in ceremony

Ambani ji sat in the first row
with Nita & beta & Sadhguru.
When Modi ji entered he went
straight to stage. Both couldn't
openly let on they were fond.
But when no one was looking,
their eyes met each others', some
say like lovers & some say like
brothers, but some said that it
went quite beyond, what they
shared was almost spiritual—
SBI calls it an electoral bond.

(Rashtrapati Bhavan, 2019)

Namesakes

(At the 'Sperm Park' opposite AIIMS)

On the second date he asked,
'What does your name mean?'
'It means the whole universe,
all of it, the whole damned thing,'
I said, quite tipsy and elated, but
found myself very soon deflated.
'Akhil,' he said—being creepy—
'isn't that the first word of ABVP?'

फासीवाद की सबसे पहली देन होती है

घटिया कविता

कनॉट प्लेस के बीचो-बीच
नयी दिल्ली नगर पालिका
ने कविता सम्मेलन आयोजित किया

काफी ताम-झाम

स्टेज के बीच इक टिप-टॉप गद्दी पर
कोई आचार्य जी विराजे
—बस एक कमंडल की कमी—
उनके साथ कोई केंद्रीय मंत्री,
लेट आये, बिठाये गए

दो-चार गुलदस्ते दोनों को थमाए गए

उनके इर्द-गिर्द दस-बारह पट्टे-कवियों
की पूरी अनुशासित सीटिंग

और फिर क्या
ताल, लय, शब्द की फुल रेढ़ पीटिंग

MP से आये एक युवा कवी
ने माइक संभाला

पहली चार लाइनों में ही
कश्मीर, परमाणु बम, पाकिस्तान, जंग
सब कह डाला

श्रोतागण ने ताली मारी, उन्होनें स्वीकार किया
पीछे मुड़ मंत्री जी को सलाम ठोका,
चापलूसी की हद थी,
उसको पार किया

माइक छोड़ने का मन न हुआ
तो दो-तीन BMKJ का आवाहन किया

फिर वापस सीट पर गए
अंडरवियर दरार में फस गया था
हलके से, किसी के देखे बिना, निकाला
बुदबुदाए 'जॉकी साला'
पर बाहर से मुस्कुराये

फिर उनके बाद अगले चाटुकार आये

'Minuscule minority, Minuscule minority'

—the judges kept on barking,
clearly they've never been
on a Sunday evening, to the
park above the Palika parking.

(2013)

i want to 377 you so bad

till even the sheets hurt i want to
ache your knees singe your skin
line you brown breathe you in i want to
mouth you in words neck you in red
i want to beg your body insane into sepals
i want to 377 you like a star falling off the brown
i want to feel you till my nails turn water
i want to suck you seven different skies
i want to be a squatter in your head when
it sleeps when it's dark i want to break laws
with you in bed and in streets and in parks

(Kashmere Gate ISBT, 2013)

Girl, when you

blow your boy,
or boy, when
you go down
on her, or when
both of you use
a toy, and all the
world's a blur,
I know it feels
like heaven, you
too violate 377.

(2014)

[Varun is Typing]

Varun: ~~Hey how have you been? You know just last week I had been thinking of you~~
Varun: ~~Listen hey I'd been meaning to tell you something for a while but~~
Varun: ~~Hey I saw you near PVR Saket the other day and I was going to~~
Varun: ~~Hi Uday, have you seen *Margarita with a Straw*, Would you want to go this week?~~
Varun: ~~I don't know how to say this but I'm just going to,~~
Varun: ~~Hiiiii~~
Varun: Hi

[Uday is typing]

Uday: ~~Hiiii I'd just been thinking about you, where have you been~~
Uday: ~~Hellooooo you, long time!~~
Uday: ~~Varun!!!~~
Uday: ~~Hiiii, you know I saw you near PVR Saket the other day and was going to say hi but~~
Uday: ~~You know you have a long life, I was just~~
Uday: Hi

निज़ामुद्दीन वेस्ट के 'स्टार लुक्स' सलून में

वो दौड़े दौड़े आया और बोला: 'भाई, बहुत जल्दी में हूँ, बस एक्सप्रेस-ट्रेन की तरह शेव बना दो,' तो इसपर नाई ने चुटकी लगाई, बोला 'जल्दी तो करूँगा पर कुछ बाल जरूर रह जायेंगे, फिर न कहना कि तुम्हें अच्छी शेव नहीं करनी आती है, क्या है कि एक्सप्रेस ट्रेन हर छोटे-मोटे स्टेशन पर रोकी नहीं जाती है।'

Things you discover your first day cycling in Delhi

Cars are beasts.

You are tiny.

But sometimes, near red lights,
you can outrun the best of them.

Cycle lanes change everything.

The Ring Road
takes almost ten seconds to cross
widthwise, and a lifetime to go around.

Working-class cycles
do not have helmets and lights
and their main purpose is not 'exercise'.

From the Def Col nallah
to the under-the-flyover Saheli office
is a slight dhalaan you hadn't noticed before.
Now it comes as a welcome surprise.

You discover the inclinations
of your city—where it nods,
where it raises an eyebrow.

That from the ITO metro station
to the Medical College is a slight chadhaai.

You always pay for a *dhalaan*
with a *chadhaai* somewhere else.

Things slow down.

As you cycle you notice
puncture shops near your home,
one opposite DPS Mathura Road,
one at the railway tracks at the Lajpat station.

With such time, you look at things closely—
at Modi posters, at his Madame-Tussauds trimmed beard,
at funeral processions, at bathing men,
at hypno-Kejriwal.

Rickshaw-pullers ask you
to move it.

Near Pragati Maidan, a boy
looks out his school bus window

with a cocky class 3A sort of smile—
'Uncle, aapke paas motorbike nahin hai?'
'Nahin.'
'Isme gears nahin hain?'
'Nahin.'
'Simple?'
'Haan,' and looks somewhere
between disappointed and amused,
till an older boy pulls him down.

Bus drivers that let you pass
deserve a place in heaven.

At 11 Ashoka Road,
in the giant party posters,
Atal Bihari Vajpayee and L.K. Advani,
though top-left, feel like bottom-right.
Remembering the old days,

you cycle past them
as Lutyens' trees open their arms.

That evening

in Kamani,
—we went for
a Hamlet adaptation
as the sky outside had rained grey—
and the actor playing Fido (Polonius)
had said—'Imagine Gertrude,
all of us will die, everyone today
sitting in this theatre
will one day be gone. All
of them.'

Outside in the lobby
as we waited to be ushered in,
I knew three faces in the crowd.
Two were old students
and one was a woman who on the metro once,
fortyish, spectacled,
had asked me about the book I had on my lap—
Dorothy Parker's *Enough Rope*—
she had said *her poems are so clean.*
She stood near the door now
holding her ticket,
by herself, a face that I had once seen.
(Gertrude: What will the next century look like, Fido?
Fido: It will be, Gertrude, unfamiliar.)

That evening
in Kamani, as the DMRC cranes outside
dug deeper into the ground,
the understudy stole the show,
walked on air, an' ended his song—
after the music, after the ball,
a cold ground awaits us all.
The idea is so *neat*—all in the audience
will be gone, nothing
could be easier than this, nothing
was simpler than this,
this—our doing the rounds—
old students, old friends.

There was a standing ovation
(the actors did not come twice for the bow)
and, at the end, moving out—
no ground beneath our feet, in the crowd
I once again spotted her, on the stairs
(*should I go and say something?*)
and before I decided, on the last step
she had turned to me,
her spectacles hanging on her neck,
and said 'Dorothy Parker!' and I felt,
at that moment, somehow, that I could embrace her,
even in this crowd, even in this city, if only I tried—
both of us will one day be gone.
A whole world lies in the goodbye,

and no matter what you tell me, Fido,
Gertrude had said,
I don't want to die.
I don't want
to die.
I don't
want to die.

(thanks to Rajat Kapoor)

Ghazal

That Srinagar bed—hours—we spread to each other,
in our kiss—years—all that was unsaid to each other.

Even broken promises are worth holding on to;
break promises like rubies and give red to each other.

Stars aligned like a prayer or a cursed constellation,
what was it that night when we were led to each other.

Death lends grace to love, a silent indemnity,
no more fear of what we could have said to each other.

Your voice, now forgotten, was the last to go,
it's silent now, that amethyst night we read to each other.

Akhil, what did you give to him, what did you get?
My heart for his. *That's it?* And head to each other.

Nigambodh ghat

As we step out
the ashes from the fires
slowly settle on us.

We are carrying back
the dead.

The chandelier in Jama Masjid

Pendulous iridescence

knotted arcs
of refraction

gold-rimmed
resilient

soap-opera
hanging from the ceiling

its weight
held entirely by sandstone
and the takbir

light, its willing prisoner,
squatting in thousand crystal cells
reflecting the world
— *Jahan-Numa*—

its crystal holds in its glass
the marble tulip
realised above on the old dome

another reflects a boy
folding the Maghrib prayer-mat
patterned in stone

another holds light, long-travelled,
finds horses tied to the Masjid corridors
—now a British barrack—
in those years of jagged insult
after the sepoys had nailed
on its walls an audacious dare

mutinous, like 'love occurring
in the middle of…terrifying air'

till another glass refracts
the gallows—not far, not
long after—bearing a crop
unseen in September

this is heavy, luminous
register, this is incandescent
record

in '47, Azad listens
to the stone-longing
of its minarets—*hamein kiske
rahmo-karam par*, at whose mercy
are you leaving us?

this is faith encased
in glass, this is leaden longing

God's pendant

rain of mercy
that is falling

that has always been
falling

(thanks to Habib, Safvi, Baldwin & Aziz)

Jama Masjid
(2012)

'Aman ♥ Rekha'

cut into the farthest edge
of the minaret.

See how love
happens
only

at the most precipitous places.

In Delhi, last winter

we needed a photograph
for the poster of your talk
Women's Movements in Post-War Sri Lanka
so you suggested—

'Take any from my FB album
in which I am wearing enough clothes
and not making a face,'

which took my choice from hundreds
to about two.

We chose you in purple,
smiling, sitting against a wall in JNU,
taking the piss out of us.

(You requested signatures
for petitions with 'Where the hell
are your endorsements, bitches?')

You are wearing a silver hoop
in your ear, the joke you just cracked
has diminished the Delhi sun,
each crease in your kurta
is already becoming memory.

After looking at this photograph
many times over I know
why your name meant 'loved'
I know why this memory is silver, I know
why this memory will now always be silver.

('... pack your best clothes,
Priya would have hated any of us
badly dressed for the funeral.')

Priya,
I have three winters
and terrace nights and songs with you
I have a midnight dance with you
and because you thought we 'Indian fuckers'
were 'too dramatic', I will, for your sake
keep safe in my hands,
all the evenings
that won't let you go.

(for Priya Thangarajah, 1982–2015, Sri Lankan feminist, queer and democratic rights activist and lawyer)

Sappho in Delhi

My metro pass, I lent her. She went
wherever her whim sent her.
Back home at night she held me tight,
said 'You never told me, you fool,
that y'all are this damn cool,
'Violet' and 'Pink' and 'Magenta'?
The DMRC has a Lesbian Agenda!'

Limerick for the danger boy

Aditya from Khanpur who was 19 sped
his auto so breakneck I bet I'd be dead
so I thought I'll talk, that'll slow him
'Kab se chala rahein hain?' to bore him
'Aaj hi learner's mila hai!' he said.

At the tailor's
(Kamla Nagar)

you slip off your shirt
so casually

not knowing
my fingers are
breaking into bits

seeing you
try on clothes

I hope nothing fits

no silk
is worth this skin

as blameless as glass
as brown as sin

I am undone

you try one
after another

every button you undo
a drop of gin.

Whenever you see it

'… the sun is always eight minutes old.'

The laughter track in the American sitcoms
was recorded in the '60s.

So whenever you hear it,
it is mostly the dead laughing.

The wrinkles on your skin
are things you could not say
but have kept for others to see.

The past is only a quarrel
and a missed phone call
and a bagelshop on 117th street.

Near the ITO, when he said—'night charge extra,'
I already knew how the night always extracts its price

how—in the 6×12 solitary cell,
as nights stretch,
flags of all countries are always red.

This world, Alfred, is only as big as your room
and grief is, finally,
only a rhyme scheme

converting separation
into a.b.b.a

and love
—*the old masters, how well they understood*—
is a tulip that flowers for three days.

(thanks to Agha Shahid Ali, Paromita Vohra and W.H. Auden)

हर रात

उनके ख़्वाब में
एक ट्रेन स्टेशन से चलती है

आहिस्ता-आहिस्ता, एकदम खाली,
न कोई उतरता है,
न चढ़ता है

लोग सोचते हैं
ज़िन्दगी के आखिरी लम्हों में
आखों के सामने क्या आता है

इतने सालों पहले
जुनैद की माँ को अभी से मालूम है

(हाफ़िज़ जुनैद खान, 2003–2018, के लिए, बल्लभगढ़)

रामजस के मेरे एक शिक्षक मित्र बता रहे थे

कि हाल ही में दिल्ली विश्वविद्यालय के छात्रों और शिक्षकों को
जब ABVP ने पीटा, तो उनमें से एक कार्यकर्ता ने
सबको देख कहा 'अरे यार इनमें से आधे तो छक्के हैं।'

यू.पी. के इक्कीसवे मुख्य मंत्री योगी आदित्यनाथ ने
कुछ साल पहले गोरखपुर में अपने समर्थकों से ये कहा
कि मुसलमानों के खिलाफ लड़ाई में केवल ताकतवर
ही हिस्सा ले सकते हैं, कोई शिखंडी या हिजड़े नहीं।

कहानी की सीख—इस दौर के शिखंडी बनो। उनकी
मर्दानगी को ठुकराओ। छक्के बनो। ताकत की इस गलत
व्याख्या को अस्वीकार करो। जिनसे लड़ने को कहें उनसे
प्यार करो। हिजड़े बनो। नफरत पर धिक्कार करो।

(2017)

For JNU

You can chew the sun here & spit it out
You can make the mighty eat dust
It's a university that we're talking about
Not a king's court where we must.

(February 2016)

दुआ, इन दिनों

सोच में आज़ादी हो,
प्लेट पर खाना हो,
किस्म-किस्म के लोगों
का आना-जाना हो,
बात-चीत हो बहस में,
प्रेम हो, क्रोध हो, जिज्ञासा
हो हर रहस्य में, नाचना हो,
गाना हो, पन्नों में लिपटा हर
ख़याल हो पुस्तकालय में,
विश्व हो विश्वविद्यालय में

Delhi summer

Light melts in slow drops.
Amaltas.

(Karol Bagh, 2015)

Behind the Lodhi crematorium

in the tin slats of the enclosure that keeps firewood, runs the Barahpullah. Ash falls on the cars. The dead travel back to us. We wait for the priest to finish the prayers. The body waits for us. There is an Urdu word *pazirai* which Shakir used to describe how she was first loved by him, like fragrance is quietly received by the air. Pazirai is the receiving. The evening descends on us like this word. The electric cremation though less brutal than the fire has the trenchant clang of metal against metal before the body is jutted in. A prayer leaves us. As we walk back the smoke divides the skies into columns. We are silent. The ash is falling on all of us. After the couplet for those days of love, where she let the soft audacity of pazirai happen, Shakir refused to speak of him. Frangrance disperses. He left like he had loved. A memory of scent on the wrist. This evening is the word she had found for the love before its inevitable going. The dead are always spreading inside us.

(after Parvin Shakir)

The funeral
(Nigambodh Ghat)

Rohit has forgotten to iron his kurta,
even on a day such as this.

Didi has a handkerchief
constantly stuck to her mouth to stop the tears.
I hope she knows she looks ridiculous.

Usha aunty is being a good neighbour
and speaking to the priest about the next ritual.
Always the practical one.

I'm surprised Apoorva has made it.
It's been years.

Papa has not shed a single tear.
He is standing in one corner
refusing to believe it still.

When the priest asks him
he lends his shoulder to me.

I can feel the nearing heat of the furnace.

Half an hour

(October 2013)

It was the first winter rain,
the auto stopped
at every red light.

When I told him
my friend had passed away,
he had asked—'Was she married?'
'No.'

At the Lodhi crematorium,
as the fire took her—outside
it was still raining—our hugs
were longer,
warmer.

'No one knows the ways of time,'
the auto-guy had said, and
I had thought that there is repose
today even
in this.

Betu, I had read about her
before I met her—'Sangini support meetings
are held every Saturday afternoon, from 3 to 6,'
the brown poster had read.

In the dusty
first-floor Santa Cruz library,
I took notes for my dissertation.

'These meetings are open
only for lesbians, bisexuals,' the solid font said,
'and women exploring their
sexual orientation.'

Betu, who I met 3 or 4 times,
who I still knew best as that paragraph
in my thesis, and of whom someone said that evening,
'I had no friend like her'—leaving that page,
leaving her—now Betu is gone.

The priest only told us, 'It takes less
than half an hour for the whole body to burn.'

On the way back
on the Ring Road, as the auto-guy
refilled the CNG tank,
I sat on a concrete bench outside.

Nearby, a palash tree almost knelt
to the ground.

It is still raining.

Indra Vihar
(2012)

I come back home switch on
the geyser put the tea to
simmer take a bath
prepare dinner
eat I do not
kiss you

I give my mother a call put
aside clothes change
the sheets lock the
doors lie try to
sleep I do not
miss you

No one knows there's a sharp precipice

where you turn on the Mall Road
for Indra Vihar

each time I pass
I balance slowly on its edges

cars go by as if there were a road
over the abyss I see

people pass as if walking over craters
was their daily commute

no one will believe me
when I tell them a canyon eats into my earth
in this part of the city where
you and I last spoke

where evenings are still sucked into its gulf
with a whiplash

and I walk out of myself to fall again
and again

what if one day my whole city falls into
your voice

Outer Ring Road

you're in an auto
speeding

he's standing by the roadside

you hold only a glimpse
before a bus passes between him
and you

your neck keeps turning on an axis
of desire

the bus consumes all angles

passes by
leaving nothing of him

leaving everything of him
you keep moving

still holding
the glimpse

you will hold on to
all year

Twenty kinds of people on the Delhi metro

There're the creepy gawkers,
the loud talkers, the just-as-
the-gate-closes-rushed walkers,
the man-spreaders that go that
way & this, the sleepers who miss
their station and reach Mundka or
Mujesar (someone wake them!),
then those crazy door-hoarders
who wouldn't leave it though their
station's far, the mirror-gazers
always checking themselves out
in the window-bar, the smart-
-phoners, and those with book-
-boners & the UPSC preppers
mugging the capital of Ukraine,
then those who get on the wrong
train, and having entered ask,
and those who bask in telling them
they're wrong, then those couples
who stay in long inside metro stations
(the only place they can meet),
and those who pretend to sleep
when they don't want to give up

their seat, then that fleet of school
kids in the afternoons, then that
shoving variety of goons, and that
kid who gazes at all the cabin-lights
and the steel on her first ride, and
those who cruise looking either side,
and those always in a hurry, who
pant and heave, and those who,
it seems, never want to leave.

Hip-Hop boy

on Violet Line
parkour body
cypress vine
on steel rail
which in his
grip is gold.
Fuck Akhil,
you're so old.

At night, I woke up

suddenly, the ground
shook a little for, say,
2 or 3 seconds. In the
morning the newspapers
reported no earthquake.
My landlady said 'Oh that,
if you notice closely, that
happens every few minutes,
if you were to keep time.
It's between Jangpura and
Lajpat, the Violet Line.'

The road from Kishangarh

was silver-sheeted
by rain

and your words, Hoshang,
were still in the sky.

Sitting by
the open door
in a white kurta,
you had let me in.

We stood
on the balcony, eyeing them—
'We fairies are all mad,'
you said, 'we don't save money
and we're generous to a fault.'

Suffering,
now white like ivory,
you had toyed with in
your hands all these years,

books you always
let remain on the floor
and the hugs

you no longer suffered for very long,
knowing the cost,

and no matter that people had come
and gone, all your heartbreaks were your own.

The rain, on my way back,
made into quicksand the ground
I trod on, and

the radio played the song
about how, on a rainy night,
the sky sends stars to the earth

how the sky sends stars
to us.

(for Hoshang Merchant)

दिल्ली दी गे पार्टियां

किट्टी सु दा EDM ते सर दे उपरों निकल गया
पर फ़िल्मी कैफ़े दा DJ नस्सां विच्चों उतर गया
किट्टी सु दे मुंडे ते डेविड गुएट्टा करदे लयी, पर
फ़िल्मी कैफ़े दे विच्चों मुंडेया ते मुंडेया दी गल बन गयी

कदी बेब्बे जी डिग्गे, कदी बाउजी

कदी मुन्नू, कदी चुन्नू, कदी ताऊजी
पंजाबियां नू कदी सम्झ नहीं औना ऐ
इन्नानें बाथरूम इच मार्बल ही लगौना ऐ

तुम्हारी एक sight

जैसे BRT पर green light
बस सुकून ही सुकून

Memory
(DU Summer, 2007)

The sun
is mercury on my skin.

It must be you burning in.

Jangpura Extension

The Latin word for
the ear is *pinna*: wing.
I knew why this morning

as you held me between
forefinger and thumb, I
became cartilage ready to fly—

you woke, and outside
the rain made petals of
bougainvillea so heavy

that they shed, filigreeing
the pavement with the
colour of sunrise.

Later we walked towards
the stadium wading through
remnants of the sun

attenuated under our feet
the earth was *thawing from longing
into longing.* You said bye

took the metro, and I
walked on past noon.
When turning near JLN

a Maruti stopped nearby
a man, about fifty, Sikh,
asked me the directions

for Khanna Market. I told him.
He said 'Come I'll drop you.'
I said 'I'm going to Lodhi Gardens.'

Again, quieter, 'Come,
I'll drop you.' The sun
was thawing in his eyes.

'I'll walk,' I said.
He took my answer and
crushed it on the road.

(thanks to Agha Shahid Ali)

auto ride
(winter)

i'm only my lips
you're only your tongue

i'm neck
you're teeth

i'm breath
you're cheek

you're fingers
i'm spine

i wait on your words
you mine

i'm all ear, love,
but you fear love

Crossing over Yamuna into Delhi

The river is black.

The Delhi smog
dark grey

except
that moment
as the sunset bled

the sky
over Batla House
was red.

Akshardham Temple

Muslim—check
Dalit—check
Christian—check
File under 'Things to erase'

Hindu—check
Brahmin—check
Moral high ground—check
File under 'Things we will praise'

Cellphones—check
Handbags—check
Common sense—check
File under 'Things visitors must leave outside'

Food-court—check
Souvenir-shop—check
Brain-washing—check
File under 'Things visitors do besides...'

I saw him running behind the 541

It was late evening
near the ITO
I saw him running behind the 541
and as it happens whenever you see
someone running behind a bus
your heart shadows the man
and runs with him
and hopes he catches
what he is after,
and if he scores
you brighten up
for his pursuit had always been yours,
and if he falls back in his trail,
you, even sitting in that bus,
also fail.

The Barakhamba Road/Tolstoy Marg crossing
(Delhi Queer Pride)

An odd, white handkerchief tied on his arm,
he gets onto the metro at Vishwavidyalaya.

With a stuffed backpack on her shoulder,
she boards the bus at Shahdara.

In his grey track pants,
he hails an Ola from Saket.

With her phone in her back-pocket,
she climbs onto a Haryana Roadways bus.

> The red glass bangles he'd bought yesterday
> reflect the winter sun; his fingers dance.
>
> She pulls out a crumpled rainbow muffler
> and waves it to her from across the road.
>
> He sees a small tear in the stockings as he
> pulls down the track pants but doesn't care.
>
> At that Crossing she knows from the map, she
> sees a big crowd—turns her phone to silent.

This is not fair, Bombay

to get me in the habit of the sea, as if
you do not know, I am from and will go
back to my land-locked Delhi. Now the
next time I feel blue and all the world
comes crushing down on me, what do you
suppose I should do, with no sea, no
waves, no sand, no grey, wet boulders
on this calming edge-of-land, that tell you
the world's too big to carry on your shoulders,
so let it be, so let it be.

(thanks to Kyla Pasha)

When

When all the gay boys get their shit
together, go to the gym and get fit
together, I sit and generally complain
about the weather and all that,
she says—That is why you're fat!
Now, now, I say, what's the hustle,
have you had a look at my arm,
lately a tendon threatens to look
like a muscle, so be calm, and by
the way, I am very good health-wise,
twice a day, I think about exercise.

(thanks to Pramada Menon)

When she and I go together

what is it
that makes the sales guy
only speak
to her when we buy
the
curtains
for
my
house?

My guess is
it's the same thing
that makes
that silly broker think
he can
only look at me
and vent
as we try to see
a
house
for
her
to
rent.

(Lajpat Nagar & Greater Noida, 2013; for Anannya Dasgupta)

One of the last things
(2011)

'…she had a song of willow;
An old thing 'twas, but it express'd her fortune,
And she died singing it: that song to-night
Will not go from my mind'

One of the last things she dreamt about
was her classroom
but only as someplace she could not find.

'I am walking in the corridors, Akhil,
I have to take my class
but I keep on searching for my classroom,
there are so many rooms here,
and doors, but none which are mine,
I am lost in the corridors
that I have walked in all my life.'

Half waking, through that haze of medicine,
one of the last things she dreamt about
was water,
was being thirsty.

They had stopped it in her diet.
'It interferes with the kidneys,'
the doctors had said, 'it obstructs recovery'.

On the ventilator, delirious, she had told her sister,
'I have become so poor
I cannot even afford a glass of water.'

How do I claim for you, Lalita,
—tonight my eyes itch and it bodes weeping,
a sea brims in the eyes—
all this water, your wealth,
all this, while you
are sleeping.

(for Lalita Subbu, teacher extraordinaire, Hindu College)

It is two years before

I am in Delhi again.

They've made me stay
at the Gandhi guest house
for the conference.
Off the Ring Road,
behind Raj Ghat, a turn
I had never taken before.

It is that night again of two years before.
At ITO, I board the bus back
and sit on the second-last seat.

From the last row
I can hear you and me,
I am telling you he will understand,
my room-mate, come
and stay tonight.

I am trying hard to hear
but you and I are almost whispering.

It is that February night again,
of two years before.
The winter is on its last leg.

I get off the bus with you two,
keeping two steps behind.

I want to tell you, and me, to be kind
and not raise the stakes
tonight,

the night of the smallest month,
for small love.
I do not rue it, and two years before,
that winter night, I leave you two to it.

(2009)

This evening

a staccato
of concrete
punctuates a red sky

metro-pillars
—like so many
cement stalagmites—

cut the horizon
into even lozenges

sad rhombuses
drop from the sky

the road splinters
as his neck
prepares to turn

millions of headlights
behind him

like so many crushed diamonds
ready to be consumed
by suicidal queens

JNU

the library is yellow rectangles
in the dark

the babul trees
reluctantly mark our way

three girls jog past us

and the night descends
so softly on the horizon

that she and I
do not notice that years have
passed since we have
known each other

years, each
with its reckoning

till, she stops
we turn in among the babul
and walking over the
silver rocks, she says

'This is the highest natural spot
in Delhi'

'I didn't know this,' I tell her
as we move up

under us,
hurting, the Aravallis
—the first memory of this city—
begin their dry march to the desert.

(for Vebhuti Duggal)

Did you know

silk-cotton in a storm
before it rains
in Delhi is
snow.

एक इमरजेंसी का समर्थक

माना कि
अख़बार कुछ ढंग का छाप नहीं सकते
दूरदर्शन वाले कोंग्रेसी तलवों के सिवा
किसी के तलवे चाट नहीं सकते, माना कि
इंदिरा जी सभी हदों से आगे निकल रहीं हैं
पर देखिये ट्रेन तो टाइम से चल रहीं है

माना कि
लाख आदमी जेल में सड़ रहा है, माना
दिल्ली का तुर्कमान गेट उजड़ रहा है, माना
बुद्धिमत्ता संजय गांधी को देख शर्मा जाती है,
नेकी उसके सामने आकर कतरा जाती है, माना
माँ-बेटे को समझाने की हर कोशिश विफल रहीं हैं,
पर देखिये, ट्रेन तो टाइम से चल रहीं हैं

माना कि
चीफ-जस्टिस जी की रीढ़ की हड्डी नहीं है, उसके
ऑफिस में इंदिरा जी की तस्वीर से कोई वड्डी नहीं है,
माना की नस बंद होने के बाद फिर खुलती नहीं जी,
माना की जेल की पिटाई के बाद देह हिलती नहीं जी,
माना विपक्ष आजकल कैदख़ानों में पल रही है
पर देखिये, ट्रेन तो टाइम से चल रहीं हैं

Kaanwariyas are good for the night-life of Delhi

Don't you think so? Around midnight at ISBT
Kashmere Gate, which otherwise would have fallen
silent, they set up stalls and play red & orange songs.

Boys distribute water to those who are carrying holier
water on their shoulders. (Does holy water weigh more
than regular water?) Even I, on my cycle, am offered a pouch.

There are more than usual policemen at ISBT, going in
and out of urinals, perhaps because there is more than usual
cruising, because a festival is doing the rounds of the night.

Around 1 a.m. at Malka Ganj Chowk, which is dressed in lights,
in boys dancing, in groups of women sitting out late night,
a kaanwar stops me and asks me the way to Gurgaon.

(Does Shiv reside in Gurgaon?) A little away from all this,
near the old ice-factory, a few kaanwars open the dickie of their
scooter & bring out the rum, and then I guess, bol bam bam.

Many kaanwars are running a relay race, passing the Ganga
water like a baton. They are jogging with knee pads, looking out

for each other. It is, if you don't look around it, all pretty
   admirable.

The dance, the boys, the women. The late-night-ness of it.
But there is one thing this year which I've never seen before. On
   their bikes, their tempos, their trucks, apart from the saffron flag,

this time there is also the tri-colour. Racing in the air. Why does a
God need a tricolour? Why does the lord of destruction need a
   flag?
Why is the flag of a country on a pilgrimage in the hands of little
   boys?

(2016)

Near Eros cinema, Jangpura Extension

the woman from Cameroon
    greets three white girls in
        French, I hear 'Deux ans, vous?'

The rickshaw-guy from
    Darbhanga asks the Lajpat
        aunty to pay more, she makes a मुंह.

The house broker from
    Jhung, who's been here sixty
        years, finds landlords for all the new

lawyers from Lucknow or
    Chennai, or Philly or Austin.
        The shop-cleaner from Muzaffarpur

watches the billboard with
    a 50 year old hero and a 20
        year old heroine that he will woo.

The taxi-guy from Greater
    Noida is trying to find M

  Block at midnight and cursing U-
-BER. And I am walking with his
  hands in mine, feelin' here-&-now
    and also a no-where-in-particular.

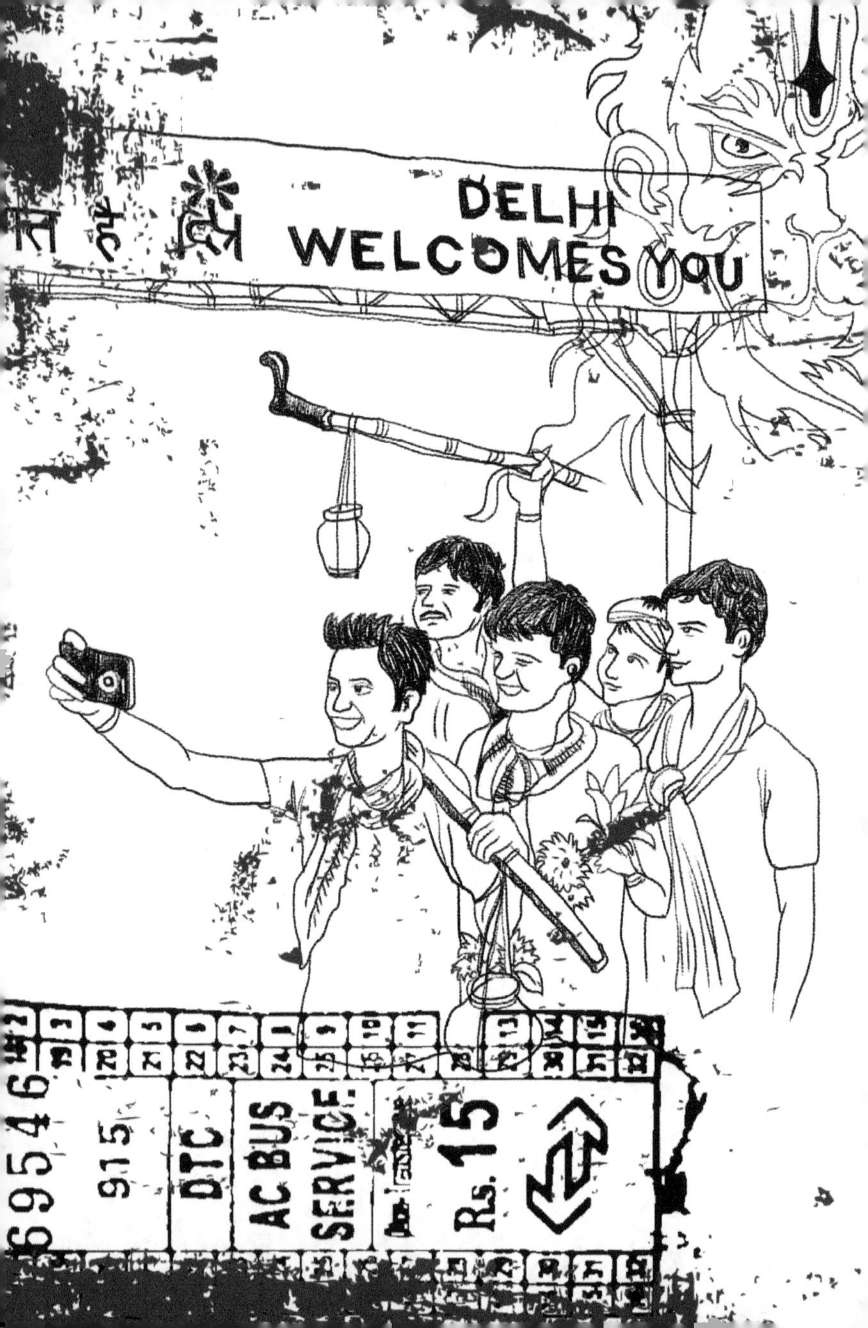
DELHI
WELCOMES YOU
915
DTC
AC BUS
SERVICE.
Rs. 15

हम हैं दिल्ली वाले जी
(खिड़की विलेज, 2014)

हम हैं दिल्ली वाले जी
हम गोरे भी हैं काले भी
जो रंग एक बतलाओगे
पछताओगे, ओ साले जी

भोगल में है अफ़ग़ानिस्तान
खिड़की विलेज में अफ्रीका है
गली गली में पाकिस्तान
तिब्बत मजनू का टीला है

'कहाँ के हो?' जो पूछोगे
किसी भी दिल्ली वाले से
हम पटना, चेन्नई, कोल्काता
काबुल से, कम्पाले से

यहाँ एक रंग नहीं जमता है
यहाँ आसमान रंगीला है
हज़ार किस्म के हम हैं जी
दिल्ली कि यही लीला है

मुझे बस

मुझे बस इक लोहे का टुकड़ा बना दे, रब
मैं उसकी बेल्ट का बकल बन जाऊं,
मुझे उसके कमरे का आइना बना दे, रब
मैं रोज़ उसकी हि शकल बन जाऊं।

मुझे रुकने का इरादा बना दे, ऐ ख़ुदा
जो मैं आऊँ तो वो ख़ुदा-हाफ़िज़ कह न सके,
मुझे घुटनों कि नरमी बना दे, ऐ ख़ुदा
मैं गुदगुदाऊँ, तो वो खुद में रह न सके।

मुझे मेरे यार का मोबाइल फ़ोन बना दे, रब
मैं उसकी पैंट कि जेब में बैठा गाता रहूँ,
जो डाले कभी वो अपनी शर्ट कि जेब में मुझे
मैं उसके दिल के करीब युं आता रहूँ।

'But he is pointing his finger at us,'

Mohit said, the guy (Thakur by caste)
as he drove me past the Ambedkar statue
on my way to work in Noida.

'One day we got together and stole
the statue in our village in Meerut
and hid it in the fields!'

'Why?' I asked.

'You see, that finger, it's always pointing
—*That* Thakur killed my brother!
That Thakur stole my land! *That* Thakur
raped my daughter, and goads our police
to use that rotten atrocity act in his book,

look!' he pointed to the one
in Ambedkar's hand,

'so we took the damn thing
and threw it away.'

He carried on speaking about the big sorrows
of the Meerut Thakurs.

I sat, quiet, seatbelt buckled,
saw the statue again, bronze Ambedkar
looked at us,
chuckled.

The railway tracks between Jangpura and Lajpat

used condoms

    empty Brislie bottles

   a packet of Lays
    crinkled like old skin
     of a robot

disused concrete slabs   that once hosted
  the parallel audacity   of railtracks

an army of polythene bags
 from Madras to Manali
  refusing to biodegrade

a listless phone charger

   recently dropped shit-pyramids
   from Palace on Wheels

rigor-mortised
cigarette-butts

    grubby plastic glasses
    huddledlikemenwhodarenotdrinkathome

injections ready to draw
        second-hand
            blood

a paper chit, half-ripped
  near the track iron
—some legible text on it
  recent, rushed like teenagers—

jab wo so jayein
to meri berth par aa jana, theek?
      'when they're asleep
    come to my berth, ya?'

आज

आज फ़ेसबुक पर तुम्हारे बचपन कि एक तस्वीर
दिख गयी। कुछ छे-सात साल के होगे, भूरी नेकर
और उसमें घुसाई हुई नीली 'हाल्फ-स्लीव' शर्ट
जो कि कोहनियों तक बेशर्म झूलती जा रही है।
हम नाइंटीज़ के बच्चे हि ऐसे बेडौल कपड़े
पहनते थे, अब देखो तो कितने भद्दे लगते हैं,
उन्हीं कपड़ों में जिनको शौक से चढ़ाए शाम को
मोहल्ले में फिरा करते थे। कॉलोनी कि मेन सड़क
पर टहलते-टहलते पड़ोसी दिख जाएँ तो 'नमस्ते
अंकल,' 'नमस्ते आंटी' करके अपने आप को बड़ा
समझदार मानते, कंघी किये हुए बालों में अपने
मम्मी-पापा का स्टेटस चिपकाए चलते और
अंग्रेज़ी के इस्तमाल से कुछ लोंगों को दबाने में
मज़े लेते। अब तुम्हारी इस तस्वीर में मुझे अपना
छे-सात साल वाला वही बेढंगापन दिखाई देता है।
लगता है इस तस्वीर के खिंचने के एक-दो दिन पहले
नाइ ने तुम्हारे सर पर एक कटोरा रख कर बाकी बाल
छांट डाले थे। इस कटोरे-कट में हस्ते हो तो बिलकुल
लंगूर लगते हो। अब ये मैं मानूं तो कैसे मानूं कि कल
रात यही बाल सवारें थे मैंने, इन्हीं को एक तरफ से
हलके-हलके दूजी तरफ किया था, और तुम्हारे साथ,
इन्हीं में मुंह छिपाए इक पूरा अरसा जिया था।

तुम आये हो

या पल्स खाते-खाते ज़ुबान पर
नमक आया है?

Flow through me

like water
through a Mughal palace,
each room slowing into a river

everywhere you touch me
becoming silver

Our phone GPS had misled us

instead of the highway
a mofussil skeleton of lanes

we reach Akbar's tomb
in a meagre, roundabout way

shadowing a ruined perimeter

each of us offering an unwitting
tawaf to the emperor.

Sikandra.
Suburban dust.
Whatever land.

Ticketed, we enter,
stubborn Delhi tourists
refusing to be impressed

and fall into the stone intarsia
of the gate.

Something escapes
our mouths.

The arabesque spandrels
of the arch mould our spines,
as if by will

and old charismatic flowers
resting in stone
halve tourists into
pilgrims.

Something relents.

Inside, even the surprise antelopes
of the charbagh do not prepare
us for the first room
of the tomb

where new gold drops into our hands
from a ridiculous ceiling.

Deep indigo drops into our eyes.

This must be the meaning of
intricate, *intricare*, we fall
into its trick.

We are beginning to surmise

ensnared

when Manucci, the old Venetian,
had first entered this 'great dome',
it was on a condition: 'make a bow
… with great reverence and
punctiliousness, just as if
the king were still alive.'

The Italian had followed,
'made a very low bow in total silence'

just as if.

Exactly as he was told.

A bare corridor slants before us
into a vault, its walls wine-smooth
with four centuries of touch.

We enter. It is cold.

This is the first time.

Bare, pendulous space. Quiet.
An old, hungry, high emptiness
heavy with cavernous air.

No lushness of marble.
No inlaid corals.

No tricks of stone.
Bare.

By abandoning all of it outside,
it stuns us into a timewarp.

Will a prayer be extracted from us
even though

this is just a sepulchre, and this is
only a grave at its centre, this is
just incense burning before us,
and these are only marigolds

the khadem, the guide—whose
name is Faheem, whose eyes are
green—uses the longevous echo
of the old chamber
for his takbir

his prayer blankets us
into its shivering skin
from all sides

there is no time left inside here
to pick on, no dust to surrender,
no sin to tell a saint

why should we touch this tomb
why should we take its blessing

something is wrong

there's no one dead here

our fingers are curling

nothing can be dead here

the king is still alive

not by the rope of a coppered *as if*
not by the excuse of metaphor
but by breath

he is here

this must be him

we turn inside and inside
our hands curving
towards each other

as if an old devotion
has made its elemental call

which we have
always known
how to answer

which our lips
have always known
how to sing

चाहने से क्या नहीं मिलता

आकाश दो तिहाई 'काश' है
आसमां आधा 'आस' है

Acknowledgements

Agha Shahid Ali gave the book its name. In his poem 'Chandni Chowk, Delhi' from *The Half-Inch Himalayas*, Shahid asked 'Can you rinse away this city that lasts/like blood on the bitten tongue?' Like several before me, I couldn't.

Karthika V.K. was as enthusastic about this book as I was. She has been a kind and a close reader.

Vishwajyoti Ghosh has brought a visual grammar to this book that does not simply *derive* from the poems, instead it *jostles* with them. For this, I am grateful.

Shrutika Mathur scanned the manuscript closely and weeded out the inconsistencies. Thank you to her.

Shikha Saklani Malviya's editorial suggestions from a previous book will always stand me in good stead. We need more poetry editors like her.

Vikramaditya Sahai, fast-walker, sari-smasher, book-guzzler, courage-giver makes this city endurable everyday. This book is for you, Vqueeram.

I am thankful to the editors of the following journals, anthologies, magazines and newspapers where some of the poems in this book have been previously published, some in earlier versions and translations:

Anti Serious: Laughter in Slow Motion; Breakups: The Mongrel Book of Voices Volume I; Contemporary Literary Review India; Culture Stories: Global Culture, Local Stories; Daily O; Feminist Dissent; Firstpost; Guftugu; GQIndia; Hindustan Times; Himal; Inklette; Lapis Lazuli: An International Literary Journal; Livemint; Orinam; Plainspeak; Scroll; Shahjahanabad: The Living City of Old Delhi; The Enchanting Verses Literary Review; The Ghazal Page: The International Journal of English Language Ghazals; The Missing Slate; The Quint; The Times of India; Vagabomb; Vayavya.

Some of these poems have also appeared in slightly different versions, in my previous books of poems *How Many Countries Does the Indus Cross* (The (Great) Indian Poetry Collective: 2018) and *Night Charge Extra* (Writers Workshop: 2015).

The Poet

Akhil Katyal is a writer based in Delhi. His second book of poems *How Many Countries Does the Indus Cross* (2019) won the Editor's Choice Award from The (Great) Indian Poetry Collective. He translated Ravish Kumar's *Ishq Mein Shahar Hona* as *A City Happens in Love* (2018) for Speaking Tiger. He has co-edited *The World that Belongs to Us: An Anthology of Queer Poetry* from South Asia (forthcoming 2020) for HarperCollins India. He was the International Writing Fellow at the University of Iowa in Fall 2016. He teaches Creative Writing at Ambedkar University Delhi.

The Artist

Vishwajyoti Ghosh is a designer, artist and graphic novelist. Author of the graphic novel *Delhi Calm* and *Times New Roman and Countrymen*, a visual book of contemporary classified postcards, Ghosh is also the curator of *This Side That Side: Restorying Partition*, an anthology of graphic narratives on the Partition. Ghosh lives and works in Delhi.

From
Arpita Singh's water colours, Sudhir Patwardhan's Bombay, Edward Hopper's America, Anupam Sud's melancholy and Iqbal Geoffrey's energy, from the pictures in the public domain, words on the walls—I stitch my new Delhi, the only city I think I know.
    Nothing original about it.

And
even if there is,
it's all forgotten, layered and even exotic
like old Delhi.

(and this is no poetry)

www.ingramcontent.com/pod-product-compliance
Lightning Source LLC
LaVergne TN
LVHW010327070526
838199LV00065B/5678